*This blessed plot, this earth,
this realm, this England*

SHAKESPEARE, *Richard II*

SHAKESPEARE'S
Town & Country

DESCRIBED BY LEVI FOX
Director of the Shakespeare Birthplace Trust

*Jarrold Colour Publications, Norwich, in association with the Shakespeare
Birthplace Trust, Stratford-upon-Avon, England*

INTRODUCTION

Stratford-upon-Avon, with the surrounding countryside, exercises a fascination almost as universal in its appeal as Shakespeare himself. It is an area which, quite apart from any literary associations, possesses a natural, historical and architectural heritage of an unmistakably English character.

Situated, as it were almost symbolically, at the heart of England, Stratford-upon-Avon enjoys a delightful river setting roughly midway along the course of the Warwickshire Avon. Originating as a river-crossing settlement, the site of Roman and Saxon occupation, Stratford has always been an important focus of roads and has served as the market centre of the surrounding countryside since the grant of its market in 1196 and its subsequent recognition as a place where fairs were held. During the Middle Ages it had a flourishing guild and in 1553 became a self-governing borough. Visiting the town in Queen Elizabeth I's time, Camden described it as 'a proper little mercate [market] towne', and it is on these lines that it has developed. Today it has a basic population of some 20,000 people.

Apart from its position as a tourist centre, present-day Stratford has a miscellany of small, light industries such as the making of engineering components, road signs and aluminium goods; fruit canning and various crafts and trades associated with agriculture and market gardening; printing and farmers' insurance business. Nevertheless, its essential rôle is still that of a market centre providing facilities for the sale of produce and cattle from the surrounding countryside. Its weekly market and shops cater as much for the needs of the countryfolk from round about as for the resident townspeople and visitors, while its annual mop fair is the survival of the old hiring fair at which farm workers offered themselves for hire.

Physically, the town preserves many links with its interesting past. The compact, well-ordered layout of the central streets, as well as the street names themselves, have altered little since the fourteenth century; the fine stone bridge that carries all the road traffic across the river was built nearly five centuries ago, and the brick bridge nearby recalls an early nineteenth-century railway project; the fifteenth-century range of guild buildings comprising chapel, guildhall, grammar school and almshouses, remains intact; while a goodly number of timber-framed homes of Elizabethan and Jacobean date survive side by side with brick buildings of later periods. The architecture of

Left: Warwick Castle.

the town is a pleasing medley of styles, the predominant tone being set by the half-timbered style of Shakespeare's day.

It is, however, the fame of the properties associated with William Shakespeare and his family administered by the Shakespeare Birthplace Trust and the Shakespeare productions centred on the Royal Shakespeare Theatre, that make Stratford-upon-Avon a Mecca for visitors from all over the world. The Shakespearian properties comprise the poet's Birthplace itself, Anne Hathaway's Cottage, the early home of Shakespeare's wife, the foundations and gardens of New Place (where Shakespeare died), with Nash's House adjoining, Hall's Croft where Susanna Shakespeare lived with her husband, Dr John Hall, and Mary Arden's House, the home of the poet's mother, at Wilmcote. At the Royal Shakespeare Theatre the poet's plays are produced nearly all the year round to an audience representative of practically every civilised nation.

The area lying within a radius of some fifteen to twenty miles of Stratford, popularly known as the Shakespeare country, is predominantly rural. The city of Coventry to the northeast is the nearest large industrial and population centre. The city and its cathedral suffered heavy bombing during the war, but major redevelopment has now produced a new city centre as well as a new cathedral and other buildings of modern design.

Between Coventry and Stratford lies the historic town of Warwick, dominated by its medieval castle, the ancestral home of the Earls of Warwick. This unspoiled county town also possesses fine period buildings such as Lord Leycester's Hospital and the splendid Church of St Mary. Two and a half miles distant but now almost linked with Warwick is Royal Leamington Spa, a fashionable resort in Regency days. The charming atmosphere of its elegant heyday still lingers on and its broad tree-lined streets offer a welcome to the visitor. Nearby Kenilworth, immortalised in Sir Walter Scott's historical novel, is also famous for its ruined castle, demolished by Cromwell's men during the Civil War.

A few smaller towns are dotted across the Shakespeare country, such as Henley-in-Arden, an old market town with an unusually long, fine main street containing a great variety of English architecture; Alcester, a small town of Roman origin situated at the confluence of the Rivers Arrow and Alne; Evesham, a riverside market town, centre of the Vale of Evesham fruit and vegetable growing industry; and Shipston-on-Stour and Chipping Campden, both small market towns on the border of the Cotswold country. In between these larger settlements lie miles of rolling fields and woodland interspersed with tiny villages. It follows that the occupations of the thinly scattered population are predominantly agriculture, market gardening and rural crafts, with relatively little light industry.

The Shakespeare countryside is notable for its quiet, varied scenery. Essentially an irregular fertile plain, watered by the River Avon and its tributaries, its gently undulating surface affords a panorama of green meadowland and cultivated farms, mixed with scattered woodland, parks and orchards. There are some scenes of great beauty: the picturesque Vale of the Red Horse as seen from Sunrising Hill; the Avon at Guy's Cliff, Stratford, Welford or Bidford; Warwick Castle from the bridge; the Vale of Evesham with its carpet of fruit blossom in spring time; Compton Wynyates in its majestic setting, Charlecote deer park; and the villages with traditional claims to Shakespearian associations.

This part of rural England, much of it formerly covered by the Forest of Arden, can best be appreciated, as it was by Shakespeare himself, in spring:

> *When daisies pied and violets blue*
> *And lady-smocks all silver white*
> *And cuckoo-buds of yellow hue*
> *Do paint the meadows with delight.*

The wonder of the leafy lanes, with the profusion of wild flowers in hedgerow, meadow and wood, recalls the poet's description of this kindly countryside in *A Midsummer Night's Dream*:

> *... A bank whereon the wild thyme blows,*
> *Where oxlips and the nodding violet grows,*
> *Quite over-canopied with luscious woodbine,*
> *With sweet musk-roses, and with eglantine.*

Wild banks, meadows, trees, herbs and flowers are still here, in all their loveliness, as in Shakespeare's time.

In other respects this area breathes the spirit of the past. Ancient monuments, buildings and associations link it with almost every chapter of English history. Considerable evidence of Roman occupation at Alcester, Stratford and other places has been found and part of the Roman road network still exists in the ancient Fosse Way and Icknield Street. Saxon settlements and burial grounds at Bidford-on-Avon and Stratford have yielded very rich archaeological finds while all along the Avon Valley fresh evidence of other early settlements is constantly coming to light.

In the days of the medieval barons this region was frequently the scene of baronial struggle and Evesham was the site of the battle at which Simon de Montfort died in 1265. Two hundred years later this seemingly peaceful countryside was troubled by yet more conflict, for it was at Bosworth Field, a little to the north of Coventry, that Richard III was slain, an episode of English history immortalised by Shakespeare himself about a century later.

In Tudor times Warwickshire was the scene of pageantry, as for instance when Dudley, Earl of Leicester, played host to Queen Elizabeth I at Kenilworth in 1575. This part of the country was also a frequent haunt of the Gunpowder Plot conspirators, Catesby, Tresham and Winter, and not many years later Edgehill was the scene of the first battle of the Civil War between King and Parliament. All over the Shakespeare country are reminders of this crucial period of English history – in the houses, castles, churches and local records there are countless references to the parts played by various local families and to the events that form part of the story of England's history.

But it is not only the stormy chapters of English history that can be traced through the Shakespeare countryside. Its architecture reflects the changing pattern of the English scene and the social and economic background of the people who have lived and worked here for a thousand years. Here, right in the middle of the country, local materials and local craftsmanship have produced a tradition of building in harmony with the countryside. Fine old mansions, farms and cottages, bridges, mills, inns and churches, all are here in quality.

All this, and much more, has already been said in innumerable books on the subject; but here, colour photography conveys and records through a selection of pictures of representative scenes and buildings some visual impressions of the essential character, atmosphere and charm of Shakespeare's town and country. Beneath the diversities of the illustrations that follow is a common quality. Each represents a place in the life and achievement of the English people; together they exemplify the deeply rooted, peaceful English way of life, with the ideas of order, stability, beauty and sincerity which are associated with our national character.

The Gower Memorial to William Shakespeare at Stratford-upon-Avon

THE AVON

*Thrice happy River, on whose fertile Banks
The Laughing Daisies, and their Sister Tribes,
Violets, and Cuckoo-buds, and Lady-smocks,
With conscious Pride, a brighter Dye disclose,
And tell us Shakespeare's Hand their Charms
   improved.*

From the poem *Edgehill* by the Warwickshire poet Richard Iago (1767)

The smooth-flowing Avon, a river navigable for commerce until the beginning of the last century, is Stratford's greatest natural asset. These peaceful waters pass directly by Holy Trinity Church (*below*), where William Shakespeare lies buried, and provide a beautiful setting for the many swans for which this stretch of river has become so well known. Upstream the Avon is crossed by a fine medieval stone bridge which has contributed greatly to the prosperity of this market town. Superseding an earlier wooden structure, the present bridge with its fourteen arches (*opposite*) was built at the end of the fifteenth century by Hugh Clopton, a native of the town who became Lord Mayor of London. During the

Civil War two arches of the bridge were broken down as a defensive measure, to be restored later. The bridge in the foreground (*above right*) dates from 1823 and was built to carry the horse tramway from Stratford to Moreton-in-Marsh. The rails have long since been dismantled and pedestrians now walk freely across the bridge.

On one bank of the Avon lie open meadows, while next to the Clopton Bridge on the other side are the Bancroft Gardens, originally common pasture, but now well-laid-out gardens and walks stretching along the river bank and around the canal basin which is the terminal of the southern section of the Stratford-upon-Avon Canal, now under the care of the National Trust. The canal was restored in 1964 and ten years later the upper Avon, after many years of neglect and disuse, was rendered navigable again up to Stratford. The river and canal have now become popular waterways for pleasure craft.

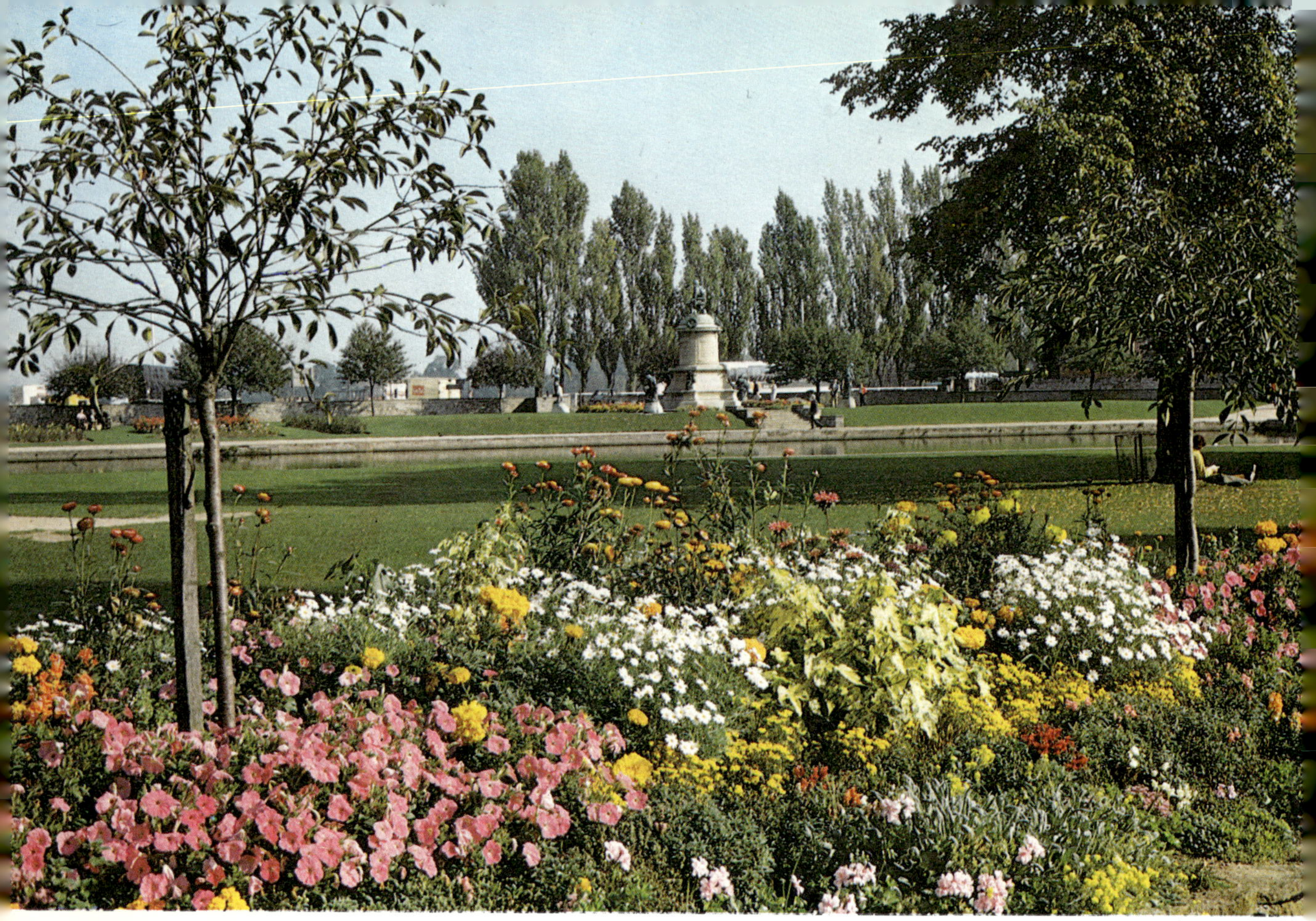

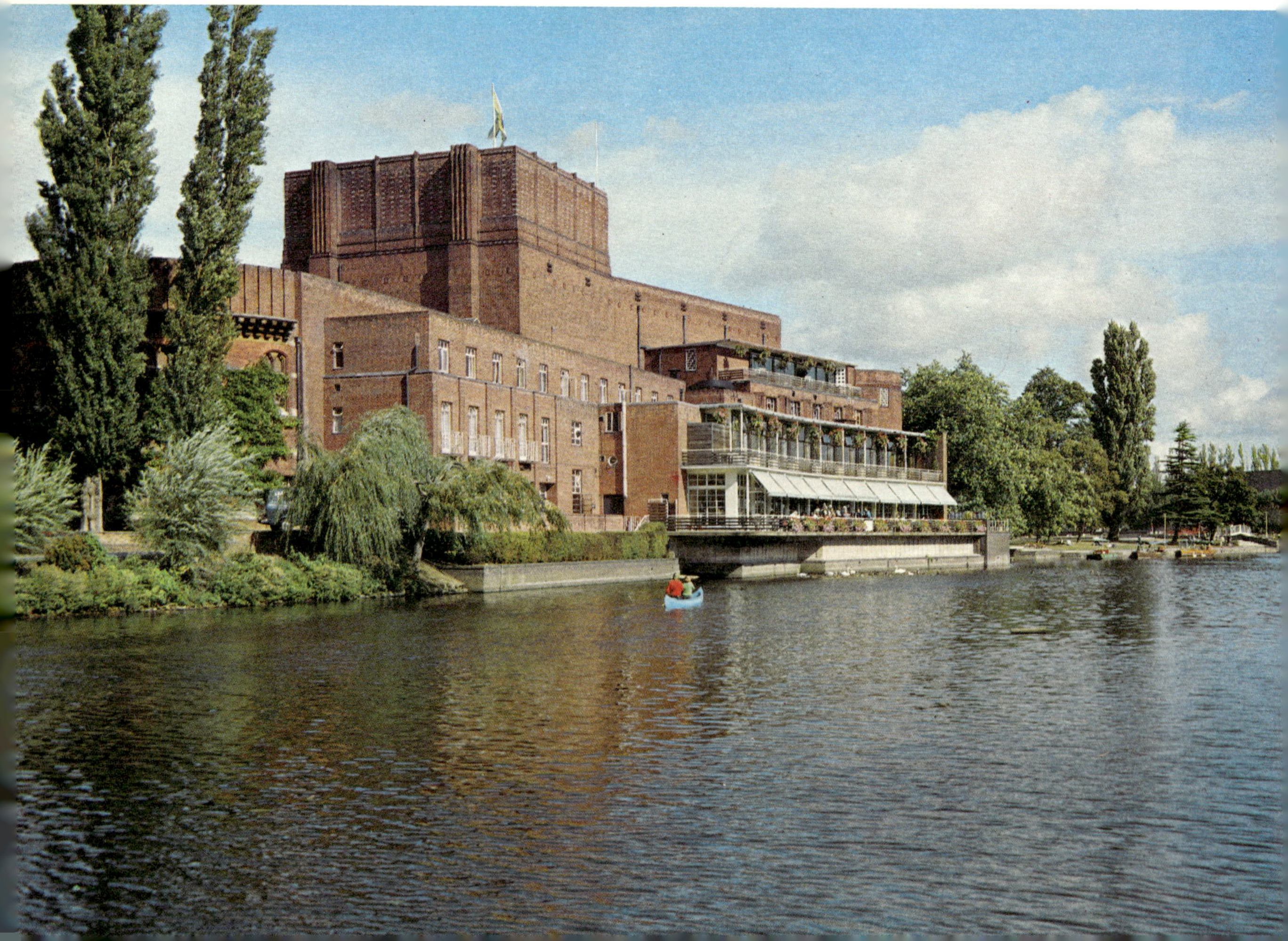

SHAKESPEARE'S STATUE AND THEATRE

Overlooking the lock and canal basin by the Bancroft Gardens stands the Gower Memorial (*left*). This imposing bronze statue of Shakespeare commands the Clopton Bridge approach to the town. The bard is accompanied by the figures of Hamlet, Lady Macbeth, Falstaff and Prince Hal. The monument was designed and presented to the town by Lord Ronald Sutherland Gower in 1888.

Stratford's first festival or celebration in honour of Shakespeare had been organised by the famous actor, David Garrick, in 1769, but it was not until 1879 that a permanent theatre in honour of the poet was opened in the town. This came about as a result of the enthusiasm and generosity of Charles Edward Flower, a local brewer, who believed that the only natural place for a Shakespeare theatre was in the poet's own town.

The theatre was destroyed by fire in 1926, but in response to appeals, funds for a new theatre poured in from Shakespeare lovers all over the world, with particular generosity from America. Designed by Elizabeth Scott, cousin of the architect of Liverpool Cathedral, Sir Giles Scott, the new Shakespeare Memorial Theatre (which became the Royal Shakespeare Theatre by royal command in 1961) was opened in 1932.

The theatre (*opposite and below*) is a remarkable example of brick architecture and was considered quite radical at the time of its building. Functional in design, its somewhat stern exterior still occasionally evokes surprise and even criticism; but as a theatre it possesses unusually fine amenities both for audiences and actors, and is equipped with all the latest theatrical devices. The riverside terraces form a particularly attractive feature of the building.

Since 1932 the story of the Stratford theatre has been one of almost uninterrupted progress. Year by year its circles of patrons has widened until now more than a third of a million people drawn from all nationalities come to see its Shakespearian productions each year. The Royal Shakespeare Company has also come to have a London home while its overseas tours have added to its international fame.

STRATFORD TOWN

When John Leland visited Stratford about 1540 he was impressed by the orderly plan of its 'very lardge stretes' and noted that the town was 'reasonably well buyldyd of tymber'. The visitor today may well form the same impression, for the essential layout and names of Stratford's streets have altered little during the past 400 years. Bridge Street (*right*) which was originally divided by a middle row of shops and houses is now a broad thoroughfare, while High Street, the main shopping street, and its continuation, Chapel Street, are notable for their wealth of half-timbered buildings.

One of the buildings of outstanding interest in High Street is Harvard House (*left*), the home of Katherine Rogers, who in 1605 married Robert Harvard of Southwark. Their son, John Harvard, was the founder of the American university which bears his name. The house had been rebuilt in 1596, following a fire, by Katherine's father, Thomas Rogers. Adjoining is the Garrick Inn and the Old Tudor House, with overhanging upper stories.

Chapel Street, so called because of its proximity to the medieval Guild Chapel contains the Shakespeare Hostelrie (*below*), another fine example of half-timbered building.

STRATFORD'S GUILD BUILDINGS

The Guild Chapel (*opposite, left*) stands on the corner of Church Street and Chapel Lane overlooking New Place and opposite to the Falcon Hotel. It was built by the influential Guild of the Holy Cross, an association of leading townsmen founded as early as 1269. The chapel was largely rebuilt in the fifteenth century, including the nave and west tower, the latter being provided by Sir Hugh Clopton, who having made his fortune as a merchant in London, where he held the office of Lord Mayor, bestowed his wealth on his native town. Above the chancel arch is a painting of the Doom or the Day of Judgement and around the walls the remains of a complete series of paintings depicting the Dance of Death have been discovered. Other remains of wall paintings are still visible.

Adjoining the chapel is a fine range of half-timbered buildings (*opposite, centre*) comprising the Guildhall, Grammar School and almshouses. 'Big School' (*opposite, top*) is one of the most interesting schoolrooms in this country. It occupies the first floor of the Guildhall built in 1416–18, which was originally the 'upper hall' used for general Guild purposes. In 1547 the Guild was suppressed by Henry VIII, but in 1553 Edward VI restored to the town the property confiscated by the Crown, on condition that it should be used for charitable and other purposes. The upper hall of the Guildhall came to accommodate the Grammar School, which had previously been conducted in the nearby School House (now known as the Pedagogue's House) and it has been continuously used for school purposes since then.

Although very little is known for certain about William Shakespeare's childhood, there is every reason to believe that he received his early education at the Grammar School. The school was maintained by the Corporation of Stratford on lines laid down by the Guild and, judging by what is known about its curriculum and masters, it must have been of very good standing in Shakespeare's day. No early lists of pupils survive, but a school desk dating from his period is preserved in Shakespeare's Birthplace.

It is also extremely likely that the young Shakespeare witnessed some of the plays produced by companies of travelling actors in Stratford during his boyhood. The earliest recorded visit of players to the town took place when his father was Bailiff and he was five years old. Such players were officially welcomed at the Guildhall (*opposite, bottom*) and the Chamberlains' accounts disclose payments made to them out of borough funds on upwards of thirty occasions. The companies which visited Stratford most frequently were the Earl of Worcester's players, who paid six visits between 1568 and 1584; the Queen's players with five visits between 1568 and 1597; and the Earl of Leicester's company, with three between 1572 and 1587.

The almshouses (*opposite, centre*) adjoining the Guildhall were erected about 1427. Now equipped with modern amenities, they continue to fulfil their original purpose of providing homes for aged local people. The tall brick chimney-stacks above the almshouses were designed to carry the sparks well away from the once-thatched roofs of the building.

SHAKESPEARE'S BIRTHPLACE

The house in Henley Street in which Shakespeare was born is a half-timbered building of a type common in Elizabethan Stratford (*below and opposite*). Like most of the houses it was a product of local materials: timber from the nearby Forest of Arden and blue-grey stone from Wilmcote. No record of the erection of the building survives, but architectural features suggest that the greater part of it was built in the late fifteenth or early sixteenth century. In Shakespeare's time the property comprised two separate parts: the Shakespeare family's home, and an adjoining shop or warehouse used by the poet's father in connection with his trade. The latter now serves as a Shakespeare museum, while the various rooms of the former are furnished in the style of Elizabethan and Jacobean times and contain items comparable to those described in inventories of the furnishings of middle-class homes in Stratford-upon-Avon in Shakespeare's day.

Records survive which prove that the property continued in the dramatist's family down to 1806, and for more than half a century before that time literary pilgrims had been visiting it. Though it has suffered some changes and necessary restoration, the Birthplace still bears substantially the same appearance as in the earliest drawing of it made by Richard Greene of Lichfield in 1769. The building consists of a low foundation wall of stone on which is erected a framing of oak beams, the spaces between the timbers being filled in with wattle and daub and the structure consolidated by a massive stone chimney-stack in the centre and a raftered roof. Though now detached, the Birthplace originally formed part of a continuous frontage of houses and shops abutting on to Henley Street. The buildings formerly on either side were demolished in 1857 to diminish fire risk.

The living-room on the ground floor (*opposite, centre*) has timber-framed walls and a raftered ceiling, which illustrate the enduring quality of English oak. The fireplace is unusual in its combination of early brick and stone and the old broken stone floor is believed to be original. Immediately above the living-room is the poet's birthroom (*opposite, top*), a fascinating apartment with a low, uneven ceiling and a quaint fireplace of stone and brick. In it is the famous window on which are recorded the signatures of Sir Walter Scott, Thomas Carlyle, Isaac Watts and other distinguished visitors to the house before it passed under the control of the Birthplace Trust in 1847.

The Birthplace makes a particularly charming picture when viewed from its garden (*opposite, below*), which contains trees, shrubs, herbs and flowers mentioned in the poet's works. Flanking one side of the garden is the Shakespeare Centre, built in 1964 to commemorate the poet's 400th anniversary.

ANNE HATHAWAY'S COTTAGE

Anne Hathaway's Cottage, the home of Shakespeare's wife before her marriage, is one of England's most famous buildings. Apart from its literary and romantic associations as the scene of Shakespeare's youthful courtship, it is a property of outstanding architectural and picturesque appeal which for generations has been a shrine of international literary pilgrimage.

It is situated at Shottery, just over a mile to the west of Stratford-upon-Avon. Formerly a separate hamlet but now linked with the town, this part of Stratford retains much of its old-world charm and atmosphere and can still be approached by footpaths over fields which were used in Shakespeare's day. Around its green clusters a group of quaint old cottages, some with half-timbered, white-washed walls, mostly thatched or roofed with uneven hand-made tiles. The row of cottages in Tavern Lane (*above*) is typical of these delightful rural dwellings.

Beyond, almost hidden round a corner down the narrow lane and beyond the brook lies Anne Hathaway's Cottage (*opposite and overleaf*), where Anne, the daughter of Richard Hathaway, was born in 1556. Her marriage to William Shakespeare took place in 1582 and she outlived the poet by seven years. At that time Shottery was little more than a cluster of homesteads on the fringe of the Forest of Arden.

Visitors are invariably impressed by the size of this picturesque, timber-framed building, with its irregular walls, high-pitched thatched roof and tiny latticed windows. It is indeed much more than what a 'cottage' is usually expected to be and this is explained by the fact that it was originally a twelve-roomed farm-house, known as Hewlands, which was the home of the Hathaways, who were a well-respected, substantial yeoman family, long established in Shottery and Stratford. John Hathaway, for instance, served as a constable of the parish in 1520 and references in records substantiate the association of the Hathaway family with Hewlands and their participation in farming activities. In Shakespeare's time farm buildings stood nearby the Cottage and some fifty to ninety acres of land belonged to the farm.

The fabric of the house, which has suffered remarkably little restoration (except for repairs following a fire in 1969), belongs to several periods. Much of it is of sixteenth- and seventeenth-century work but the oldest part dates back to the fifteenth century. Inside the house may be seen a pair of curved oak timbers or

'crucks', pegged together at the top, which was one of the earliest constructional methods used in English house building. Built on foundations of stone, the timber-framed walls consist mostly of wattle-and-daub panels finished with hair plaster inside, though in some cases brick of later date has been substituted. The central chimney-stack was rebuilt in 1697 and bears the initials of John Hathaway.

The interior of the Cottage abounds in interesting architectural features. The principal rooms on the ground floor comprise the living-room, or the 'hall' as it was called in Shakespeare's day, with its original panelling and open chimney corner; the dairy or buttery, an essential adjunct to any farmhouse; and the kitchen (*opposite below*). Formerly the scene of busy domestic activity, the kitchen is to many the most fascinating room in the Cottage. Its low raftered ceiling, stone-flagged floor and small latticed windows all contribute to its atmosphere, but the focus of interest is inevitably its wide open fireplace, originally equipped with a spit, drip pan and other cooking utensils. The oven used for bread baking is still intact, complete with its wooden 'stop'.

Upstairs there are six rooms, all formerly

used as bedrooms or storerooms, running the whole length of the building. The principal chamber lies directly at the top of the narrow stairs and is referred to in Richard Hathaway's will as his *Parlour*. In it is the famous Hathaway bedstead (*above*), a finely carved late Elizabethan joined bed. The mattress is of rush supported on cords threaded through the wooden frame, and on it is a case containing an old needlework sheet, an heirloom of the family. Leading from this room is Anne's bedroom, containing a four-poster bed of simple style with original linsey-woolsey hangings. Most of the present furnishings of the Cottage actually belonged to the Hathaways and their descendants, though a few representative pieces of sixteenth- and seventeenth-century furniture have been added.

To many, however, it is the old-fashioned garden, with the orchard adjoining, that imparts to Anne Hathaway's Cottage its special attraction. Here the smell of clipped hedges, roses and posy peas, mingles with the fragrance of herbs which Shakespeare knew and depicted so vividly; while the restful beauty of its orchard of fruit trees carpeted with wild flowers provides an almost perfect setting for this supremely English architectural gem.

NEW PLACE

Although Shakespeare spent his busy working career in London he retained his connection with his native town and once his success as a playwright was assured he returned increasingly to Stratford-upon-Avon. Having already invested money in property in London, in 1597 he purchased New Place, one of the largest houses in Elizabethan Stratford. The legal document transferring the property to the poet for the sum of £60 is preserved among the records of the Shakespeare Birthplace Trust.

New Place, standing at the corner of Chapel Street and Chapel Lane, was originally built towards the end of the fifteenth century by Hugh Clopton. Described by John Leland in about 1540 as a 'praty howse of brike and tymber', the earliest surviving drawing of it shows a large, half-timbered structure, with a courtyard in front and barns and spacious gardens attached. Shakespeare settled permanently at New Place with his family in 1610 and here he died on 23 April 1616 after entertaining Ben Jonson and Drayton, so it is said.

The poet bequeathed New Place to Susanna, his eldest daughter, wife of Dr John Hall, and it is probable that Shakespeare's widow lived with the Halls there until her death in 1623. Henrietta Maria, Charles I's Queen, stayed at New Place for three days in 1643 as the guest of Susanna Hall. Subsequently, the house was owned by Elizabeth Hall, Shakespeare's granddaughter and, after her death, it passed back into the Clopton family and was largely rebuilt by Sir John Clopton in 1702. New Place was pulled down in 1759 by the then owner, the Reverend Francis Gastrell, after a quarrel with the town authorities, but its foundations escaped destruction and can still be seen (*above left*) in this garden setting.

The entrance to the foundations of New Place is through Nash's House (*opposite*), which belonged to Thomas Nash, the first husband of Elizabeth Hall. Although the structure of the house dates mostly from the sixteenth century, the half-timbered front is a replica of the original built to replace a frontage of brick and stucco added in the eighteenth century. The interior contains much of the original timberwork.

Nash's House now serves as Stratford's local history museum containing, as well as furniture and other exhibits, local archaeological and historical material. The Romano-British and Anglo-Saxon collections illustrating early settlements in the Avon Valley are particularly fine. The various rooms give an impression of the physical background of domestic life in Shakespeare's day and there are some fine specimens of Tudor and Jacobean furnishings (*above*).

THE GARDENS OF NEW PLACE

The gardens of New Place are striking for their individual character and beauty. The Great Garden (*below*) is entered from Chapel Lane and offers an oasis of peace within a few yards of the busy shopping streets of Stratford. This garden, which is now carefully maintained by the Shakespeare Birthplace Trust as a memorial to Shakespeare, comprises the original orchard and kitchen garden of New Place. Here, where the poet must have spent many relaxing hours in his later years, the green, velvet-like expanse of lawn is no less impressive than the long borders fashioned between box and yew hedges in the formal manner of Tudor times, or the wild bank of flowers and herbs, such as savory, hyssop and thyme.

Here also stands the famous aged mulberry tree, believed to have grown from a cutting of a tree planted by Shakespeare himself. His original mulberry tree flourished for many years but, as the fame of the poet grew in the early eighteenth century, visitors wishing to see the mulberry tree became so numerous as to cause annoyance to the owner of the property, the Reverend Francis Gastrell, who in consequence had the tree cut down in 1756. When, three years later, he caused the house itself to be demolished, local indignation rose to such heights that he was compelled to quit the town 'amidst the rage and curses of its inhabitants'.

A gateway from the terrace, in the centre of which stands a sundial, leads into the Knott Garden (*right*) which has been described as 'one of the most enchanting sights of Warwickshire'. This garden, occupying part of the site of New Place, is an exact replica of an enclosed Elizabethan garden such as was invariably attached to any house of importance in Shakespeare's time, and is modelled on the designs shown in contemporary gardening books.

Square in shape and slightly sunken, the garden is divided by stone paths into four 'knotts' or beds, each of which comprises an intricate, interlaced pattern made up of box, savory, hyssop, lavender, cotton, thyme and other traditional herbs, with the interspaces filled in with flowers of many colours. The result is a 'curious knotted garden' such as the fantastical Signor Armado mentions in his letter to the king in *Love's Labour Lost*. It is a posy-like mosaic with no two beds of the same flowers together; the varied shapes and colours blending as in the garden needlework of Shakespeare's day. This delightful retreat is enclosed by a palisade which is covered with crab apples, as is also a rustic oak 'tunnell' or 'pleached bower', a popular feature in Elizabethan gardens.

HALL'S CROFT

Hall's Croft (*above*), which stands in the seclusion of Old Town a few yards from the Parish Church where Shakespeare is buried, is probably Stratford's finest surviving Tudor house. It was the home of the poet's favourite daughter, Susanna, and her husband, Dr John Hall, whose contribution to medical knowledge was widely recognised in his day.

Hall's Croft is a splendid half-timbered building built on a stone foundation with a structure of substantial oak-timber framing, lath and plaster, and with a tiled roof of many gables surmounted by picturesque chimney-stacks. The property was purchased by the Shakespeare Birthplace Trust in 1949 for preservation and part of the building is used as a Festival Club. The house is furnished in the style of a middle-class Tudor home and the parlour (*right*) contains particularly fine pieces of furniture, including an extending table which dates back to about the year 1600. Dr Hall's dispensary is equipped as a contemporary consulting room, with exhibits illustrating the theory and practice of medicine in Shakespeare's time.

One of the joys at Hall's Croft is its spacious walled garden. As the term 'croft' suggests, this was once a spacious plot attached to the house, probably comprising a garden for herbs and flowers and a kitchen garden and orchard. The garden in its present form is a modern creation, designed to portray something of the formality of gardens of Shakespeare's day while at the same time creating the intimate atmosphere of a homely garden full of familiar trees, flowers and shrubs. Much of it is now a trim lawn graced by a mulberry tree, limes, and a stately row of poplars, while herbaceous borders of old English flowers flank a paved walk leading to a sundial (*opposite*).

HOLY TRINITY CHURCH

Of all Stratford's historical buildings, none is more beautiful than the Collegiate Church of the Holy Trinity, situated in Old Town on the banks of the Avon (*opposite*). This Parish Church is at once a pleasing epitome of English ecclesiastical architectural styles and the shrine of William Shakespeare's mortal remains.

Holy Trinity Church dates in part from the twelfth century with additions in the Decorated and Perpendicular styles. The present slender stone spire replaced an earlier wooden spire in the eighteenth century. One of the most striking features of the church is the chancel; items of special interest include the door knocker of the porch, which is an old sanctuary ring, the canopied tomb of Sir Hugh Clopton who built Stratford's bridge and the medieval misericords in the choir stalls.

The most priceless possessions of the church are those associated with Shakespeare, particularly the Parish Register containing the records of the poet and his family. Shakespeare's baptismal entry in 1564 reads:

April 26: Gulielmus filius Johannes Shakspere

while his burial in 1616 is recorded in the Register as follows:

Aprill 25   Will. Shakspere gent.

The font in which Shakespeare was baptised is also preserved. Shakespeare's grave and monument, are near the altar in the chancel. The monument (*above right*), which was erected on the north wall within a few years of the poet's death, portrays a bust of Shakespeare, holding a quill pen, which was carved by Gerard Johnson, an Anglo-Flemish mason of London.

Below the monument lie the graves of William Shakespeare, his wife Anne, his eldest daughter, Susanna, and her husband, Dr John Hall, and Thomas Nash, who married Shakespeare's grand-daughter, Elizabeth Hall. The poet's grave bears the following verse:

> *Good frend for Jesus sake forbeare*
> *To digg the dust enclosed heare:*
> *Blese be ye man yt spares thes stones*
> *And curst be he yt moves my bones.*

According to an old tradition, Shakespeare himself wrote these lines, so as to ensure that his remains would rest undisturbed.

SHAKESPEARE'S BIRTHDAY CELEBRATIONS

The birthday of William Shakespeare is celebrated annually at Stratford-upon-Avon on 23 April, St George's Day. From small beginnings, designed to give local enthusiasts an opportunity to honour the memory of their great townsman, these celebrations have now assumed the proportions of an international occasion unique in its purpose and attraction. They are attended by official diplomatic representatives of the nations of the world, distinguished personalities associated with the arts, literature and the stage, and Shakespeare devotees from far and near.

The celebrations have come to follow a traditional pattern. Starting from the Royal Shakespeare Theatre the official representatives walk in procession carrying flowers and unfurl the flags of their respective countries which line the central streets in honour of the poet. The unfurling ceremony takes place in Bridge Street *(top left)* and the procession then proceeds, headed by a band, to the poet's Birthplace in Henley Street; it continues through the centre of the town past New Place and the Grammar School *(bottom left)* where the masters and boys take the head, and proceeds to Holy Trinity Church where the representatives lay their flowers on Shakespeare's grave as a tribute of homage. There follows the birthday luncheon at which traditional toasts to the immortal memory of Shakespeare and the theatre are observed and the day's celebrations are rounded off with a performance of a play at the Royal Shakespeare Theatre.

The idea of celebration or festivity in honour of Shakespeare at Stratford goes back to 1769 when David Garrick, the famous actor, organized the first Shakespeare Festival in the town. For some years after annual celebrations were held and, although these had to be discontinued towards the end of the century, interest in Shakespeare continued to increase. The tercentenary of the poet's death was commemorated in 1816 and was followed in 1824 by the foundation of the Shakespeare Club, which still exists. The festivals of 1830 and 1864 carried on the tradition and focused attention on the birthday occasion, thus paving the way for the present pattern of birthday celebrations.

THE SHAKESPEARE CENTRE

Stratford's greatest birthday gathering was in 1964 when representatives from all over the world took part in a special programme of celebrations to commemorate the 400th anniversary of the poet's birth.

The main commemorative project to mark this anniversary was the new Shakespeare Centre built by the Birthplace Trustees with the help of contributions from Shakespeare-lovers of many nations. The Centre serves a dual purpose. It is at once the headquarters of the Birthplace Trust and a study centre providing facilities for its educational and academic work. Students of all nationalities may use its specialised library where collections that Stratford has built up over the years may be found.

The Shakespeare Centre, which occupies a site overlooking the garden of the Birthplace, is a striking modern building (*above right*) described by Nikolaus Pevsner as 'a very handsome job and highly praiseworthy because so entirely uncompromising in so hallowed a spot'. Designed by Laurence Williams, the Trust's architect, the Centre is modern in conception and design but makes liberal use of traditional materials, including granite, marble, hand-made brick, bronze, wood and glass.

A bronze relief by Douglas Wain-Hobson at the front of the Centre in Henley Street symbolises the influence of Shakespeare encircling the world; and flanking the entrance, a large black granite panel, carved by John Skelton, labels the building. The entrance vestibule itself is enclosed by a series of glass panels engraved with life-size figures of well-known Shakespearian characters by John Hutton, while a bronze full-figure statue of Shakespeare provides a striking focal point in the entrance hall (*centre right*).

The reading room has the atmosphere of a large and comfortable private study, its walls being lined with individual desks, each provided with lighting and shelves. An unusual artistic feature in the form of a carved wood panel, made in five different timbers to give depth and variety of colour effect, runs the whole length of the west wall (*below left*). It is carved with the names of Shakespeare and many of his contemporaries and is the work of Mrs Nicolette Gray.

MARY ARDEN'S HOUSE

Of the many old farmsteads in Warwickshire, Mary Arden's House at Wilmcote, four miles from Stratford, is perhaps the most outstanding. Here lived Shakespeare's mother, Mary Arden, one of Robert Arden's eight daughters, before her marriage to John Shakespeare in 1557. This magnificent Tudor farmhouse (*opposite*) reflects the prosperity of the Ardens, who came of an old and leading yeoman family.

Standing back slightly from the roadway, behind a wall enclosing quaint, shaped hedges of box, the timbered frontage of the house is of striking size and proportions. Most of the building dates from the early sixteenth century, and it is built of close-timbered oak beams from the nearby Forest of Arden (mentioned by Shakespeare in *As You Like It*) and stone quarried in Wilmcote itself. At the front of the house, the upright timbers are set close together but at the back the framing is at wider intervals forming large panels (*above right*) which were originally filled in with clay on a wattle foundation. Particularly notable are the irregular lines of the building, its uneven roof of handmade tiles, with the picturesque dormer windows and the coloured patchwork of weathered grey stone, red brick and bleached timber.

It is most fortunate that continued occupation of the Arden farmstead by farmers ensured its preservation substantially in its original condition. As might be expected, some minor alterations were made, but basically there has been little change from Shakespeare's day to the present. The property was purchased in 1930 for preservation by the Birthplace Trust. It is furnished in period farmhouse style and gives an excellent impression of domestic arrangements of Shakespeare's time.

At the rear of the house, a stretch of lawn occupies the space of the original farmyard. However, the old pump (*below right*), the square stone dovecote with 657 nesting-holes built inside its walls, the cowsheds, outbuildings and barns are preserved intact. These barns, of weathered blue-grey stone, provide an ideal setting for the display of a collection of old farming implements and other 'bygones' which provide a physical link with the successive generations of people who lived in the surrounding Warwickshire countryside.

CHARLECOTE PARK

Charlecote, a magnificent Elizabethan mansion which is now one of the best known properties of the National Trust, has been the ancestral home of the Lucy family for nearly eight centuries. Its story is a cross-section of English history, focused on the activities of a family whose successive generations figured among Warwickshire's country gentlemen and left their imprint on Charlecote House and the park in which it stands.

The house is reached by a stately drive overlooked by a gatehouse, built of mellowed plum-red bricks and grey stone dressings, which is Charlecote's finest architectural feature (*above*). After 400 years, it still stands almost exactly as the builder conceived it. The mansion itself (*above right*), considerably remodelled during the nineteenth century, was built in 1558 by the famous Sir Thomas Lucy, who is said to have been caricatured by Shakespeare as Justice Shallow. Its plan, in the form of an E, is usually held to be a compliment to Queen Elizabeth I who, in 1572, was entertained here.

Charlecote stands in 228 acres of parkland situated in the Avon Valley near to the pretty village of Hampton Lucy, four miles from Stratford. Here is an area of parkland 'whose venerable verdure' to use the words of Henry James, 'seems a survival from an earlier England, and whose innumerable acres stretching away in the early evening to vaguely seen Tudor walls, lie there like the backward years receding to the age of Elizabeth.' Enclosed by a split oak boundary park, the undulating parkland unfolds like a green carpet studded with majestic elms and oaks, a perfect home for the superb herd of fallow deer (*below right*) and a rare breed of Spanish sheep first introduced by George Lucy in the eighteenth century.

One of Charlecote's most cherished associations is the legend that Shakespeare himself poached deer in the park when he was a boy. The tradition holds that he was caught red-handed and taken before Sir Thomas Lucy to be punished and that as a result of this incident the young Shakespeare left Stratford for London.

HENLEY-IN-ARDEN

Henley-in-Arden *(above)* typifies the character of Warwickshire's old market towns, and its High Street remains one of the most attractive in England. Although only one mile long, the street displays buildings of nearly every style of English architecture, ranging from gabled Tudor to red-brick Regency; with a preponderance of half-timbered buildings which are excellent examples of the work of local craftsmen using timber from the wooded Arden country nearby.

One of the finest buildings is the Guildhall, overlooked by the square tower of the parish church, which was built during the fifteenth century by Sir Ralph Boteler. It contains many treasures, including the charter granted to the town by Henry VI in 1449. There are also many ancient inns here such as the White Swan, while the shaft of the 600-year-old market cross, now protected from the traffic, provides a reminder of trading activities of former times.

Henley-in-Arden has a fascinating history: once it belonged to the de Montfort family but after the Battle of Evesham, where Simon de Montfort was slain, the town was pillaged and then burnt to the ground. Like other similar small communities, Henley-in-Arden came to have its own Court Leet, or Manor Court, which was held in the Guildhall. Here, the officials, who included the Lord of the Manor, the Bailiffs, the Ale-Taster, the Town Crier, the Butter Weigher and the two Brook-Lookers, would meet regularly to discuss and decide the affairs of the town. In 1655, for instance, they reported '... that usually heretofore there have been at Henley-in-Arden several unlawful meetings of idle and vaine persons about this time of year for erecting of May poles and May bushes, and for useing of Morris Dances and other heathenish and unlawful Customes, the observacon whereof tendeth to draw together a greate concourse of loose people.' Incidentally the Court Leet, with its traditional ceremonies, is still held each year in the Guildhall, primarily a colourful reminder of an ancient form of local self-government.

PACKWOOD HOUSE

Lovers of the countryside, garden enthusiasts, students of architecture, connoisseurs and collectors, indeed everyone who appreciates good craftsmanship and beauty, will find Packwood House an inspiration and joy. Tucked away among the country lanes between Lapworth and Knowle, this essentially English house formerly belonged to Mr G. Baron Ash who presented it to the National Trust.

The house (*above*) dates originally from Tudor times although it has been extensively restored and enlarged. Inside, the rooms are furnished with tapestries, period furniture, and Jacobean panelling; while there is some unusual leadwork on the exterior of the house.

The crowning glory of Packwood House is the yew and box topiary (*right*). The garden was planted by John Fetherstone about 1650 in a symbolic layout representing the Sermon on the Mount. There are twelve yews symbolising Apostles, four larger Evangelists and an enormous yew to represent Christ.

ASTON CANTLOW

Beyond Wilmcote lies Aston Cantlow, a pretty village in the valley of the Alne, approached by pleasant lanes. Its church (*left*), shaded by giant yews and secluded in a well-kept churchyard, has a special claim to fame, for tradition has it (in the absence of documentary evidence) that it was here that Shakespeare's parents, John Shakespeare of Snitterfield and Mary Arden of Wilmcote, were probably married. Most of the building, including the tower is of thirteenth- or fourteenth-century date.

The village itself comprises houses of different styles and periods, and includes a picturesque inn (*below*) and a range of half-timbered buildings, originally the headquarters of the parish guild. Aston Cantlow was clearly a place of importance in earlier times. The remains of a castle and of a Saxon burial ground nearby have been discovered. The surrounding countryside is still essentially rural with cultivated fields and scattered woodland.

COUGHTON COURT

An historic family mansion, now the property of the National Trust, Coughton Court is situated some ten miles from Stratford in the lovely valley of the Vale of Arrow. Coughton belonged to the Catholic family of Throckmorton from the fifteenth century, and was noted by John Leland on his travels as 'a fayre maner place' with a moat (later filled in).

This great mansion (*above*) dates from about 1500, although it has been altered and extended by successive owners. The stone gatehouse, described by Dugdale in 1656 as 'that stately castle-like gatehouse of freestone' was built by Sir George Throckmorton at the beginning of the sixteenth century. For sheer beauty of proportion and excellence of design, it ranks as one of the country's finest examples (*right*).

The interior of Coughton Court contains many treasures, including some unusually interesting family portraits and Jacobite relics.

In Tudor and Stuart times Coughton was a stronghold of recusancy and was also one of the haunts frequented by the conspirators responsible for the Gunpowder Plot.

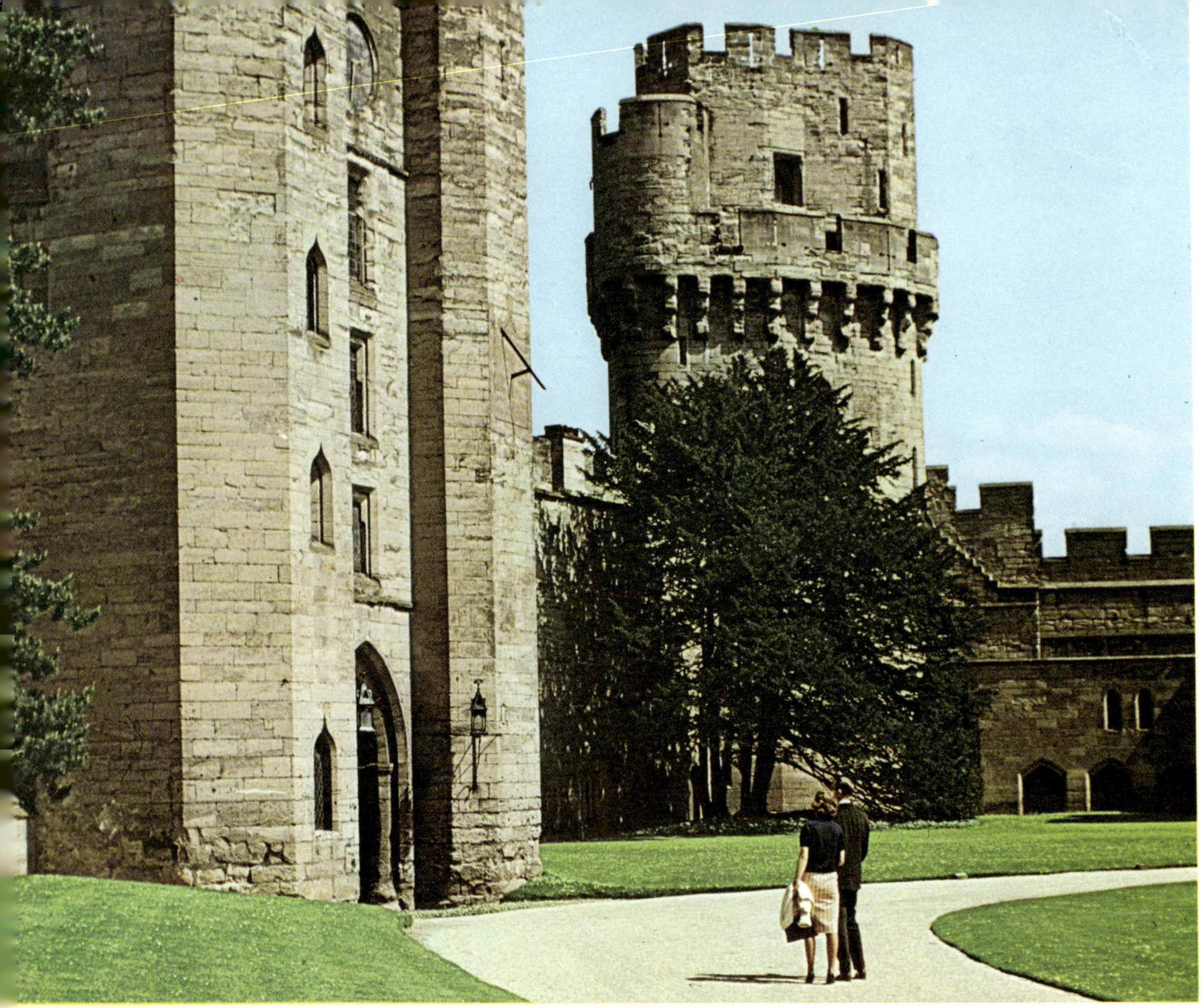

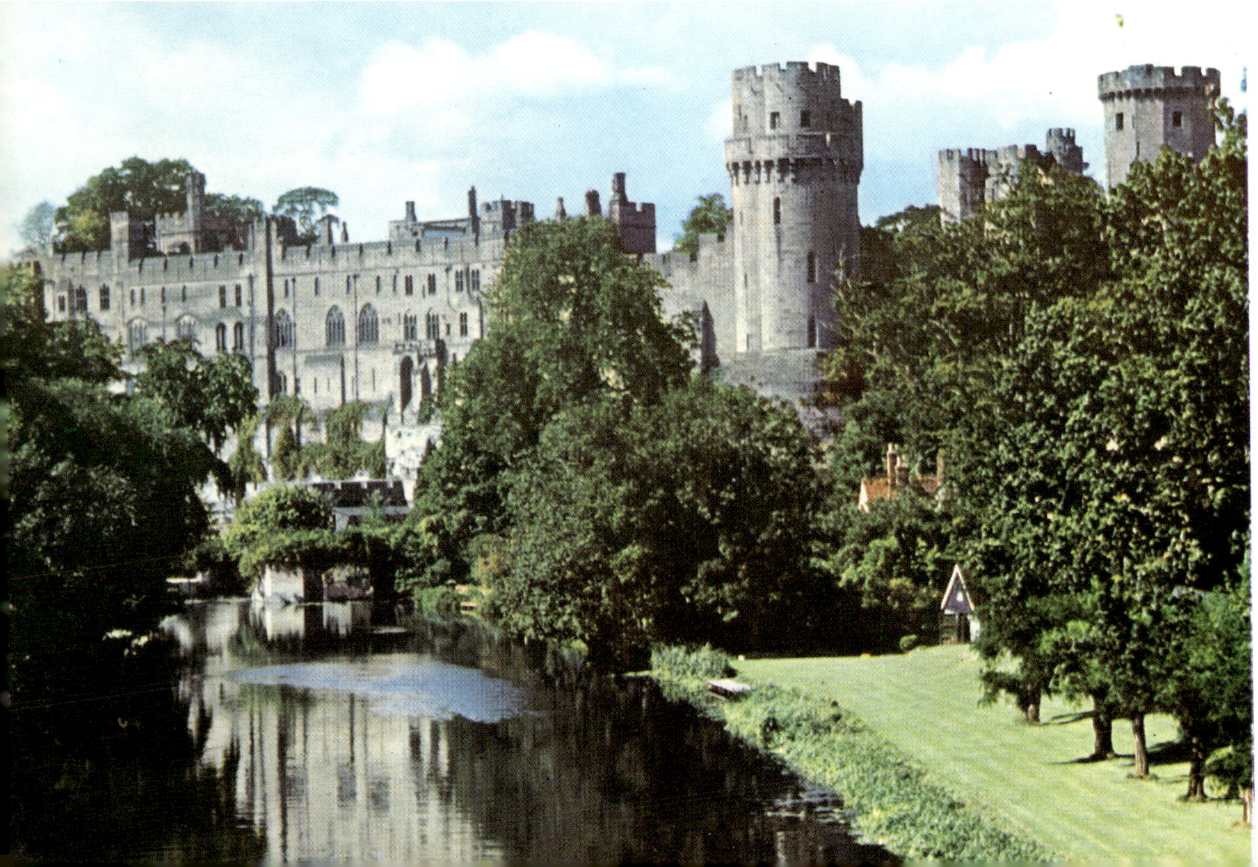

WARWICK CASTLE

Some eight miles upstream from Stratford stands the county town of Warwick with its magnificent castle on the banks of the River Avon (*below left*). Warwick Castle ranks high among the historic treasures of Warwickshire and, indeed, of England itself. It is, as Dugdale described it in 1656, 'a place not only of great strength, but extraordinary delight, with most pleasant Gardens, Walks and Thickets, such as this part of England can hardly parallel.'

The home of the Earl of Warwick, whose ancestors vitally influenced the course of medieval history (Richard Neville, better known as 'Warwick the King Maker', lived here from 1449 to 1471), the castle attracts not merely because of its architectural interest and artistic treasures; somehow it symbolises the stability and grandeur of the English heritage. It embodies at once all the features of a medieval fortress and the spacious elegance of a seventeenth-century mansion.

The fortifications of the castle are mainly the work of the Beauchamps and are dominated by their two great towers, Caesar's and Guy's, justly described as 'masterpieces of fourteenth-century military architecture'. Caesar's Tower (*above left*), the eastern tower of the castle, is 147 feet high and it commands the river crossing with imposing might. Soon after its completion, the tower was used to house prisoners taken during the Battle of Poitiers in 1356 and an unusual feature here is the *oubliette* – a dungeon within a dungeon. The towers are connected by an embattled wall which encloses the inner court. This courtyard was also protected from attackers by a deep, dry moat, made shallow now, a drawbridge and two sturdy portcullis with double doors.

The interior of the castle is magnificently furnished, particularly the Great Hall (*below*) where Piers Gaveston, favourite of Edward II, was tried and found guilty of treason in 1312. The Hall, which is 40 feet high and 62 feet long, had to be almost completely rebuilt after a fire in 1871 – the red and white Verona marble floor is laid over the original flagstones. A large Beauvais tapestry hanging on the east wall shows Marlborough's army on the march, while on the wall opposite the windows (which overlook the Avon some 100 feet below) hangs the famous portrait of Elizabeth I.

WARWICK: LEYCESTER'S HOSPITAL

Though dominated by the grandeur of its castle, Warwick is a county town of character and quality in its own right, preserving interesting links with its historic past. The town stands on a rise by the Avon and it was this prominent position that accounted for its early importance. A disastrous fire burnt down much of old Warwick in 1694, and the town had to be almost completely rebuilt.

Its buildings of architectural and historical importance include St Mary's Church, whose 174-foot pinnacled tower can be seen from considerable distances outside the town. St Mary's incorporates the Beauchamp Chapel, an exquisite example of fifteenth-century work, containing the famous effigy of Richard Beauchamp. Nearby stands the Shire Hall, an impressive and dignified building built in 1753–8.

The finest timber-framed building in the town, Lord Leycester's Hospital (*below*) stands by the West Gate, itself a reminder that Warwick was once a walled town. It was originally built for the powerful guilds of Warwick in the fourteenth century – the guild hall inside has recently been restored – and the town's affairs were virtually governed from here. Following the dissolution of the guilds by Henry VIII the property was largely rebuilt and in 1571, Robert Dudley, Earl of Leicester, the favourite of Queen Elizabeth I, gave money for it to be transformed into an almshouse for 'soldiers maimed in the warrs'.

The hospital is still run on the lines laid down by its founder and namesake, and it maintains a company of thirteen aged men – a Master and twelve 'Brethren'. Their quarters have now been modernised but the traditional Elizabethan costumes of blue cloth adorned with silver badges which are still worn by the almsmen on special occasions provide a colourful link with the past.

ROYAL LEAMINGTON SPA

Like Bath and Cheltenham, Leamington Spa, a comparatively modern town as such, has behind it the fascinating history of a fashionable watering-place. It is an attractive place, which was planned and developed in Regency and Victorian times largely due to the curative properties of its waters from the chalybeate and saline springs.

The aristocracy and even royalty (including Queen Victoria who, in 1838, granted the town the title of Royal Leamington Spa) flocked to consult Dr Henry Jephson, whose advocacy of the use of the local mineral waters brought fame to the town. The beautiful Jephson Gardens, laid out on the banks of the River Leam, and a bronze statue of the doctor perpetuate his memory.

Leamington Spa is notable for its wide, tree-lined avenues and squares, and for its terraces of Regency and Victorian houses. The Royal Pump Room (*below*), which can be seen alongside the Victoria Bridge over the River Leam, at the bottom of the Parade, is an excellent example of the dignified Regency style of architecture which gives the town such a distinctive character. The Pump Room dates from 1814, though it was rebuilt in 1925.

KENILWORTH CASTLE

Immortalised by Sir Walter Scott's novel, Kenilworth Castle is one of the outstanding ancient monuments of the Shakespeare country, interesting alike by reason of its historical associations and its military architecture. Though in ruins, sufficient of the castle remains to give an excellent impression of its strength as a medieval fortress and of its grandeur as the scene of pageantry in Tudor times.

The castle is believed to have originated as a wooden fortress built in 1112 by Geoffrey de Clinton and the keep, which can still be seen, was added by a son of de Clinton.

In the late fourteenth century Kenilworth Castle passed to John of Gaunt, who transformed it from a fortress into a princely residence. In 1563 Elizabeth I conferred it on her favourite, Robert Dudley, Earl of Leicester. Queen Elizabeth was entertained here in splendid style by Leicester in 1575. The castle was dismantled by Cromwell and the ruins are now in the care of the Department of the Environment.

STONELEIGH ABBEY

Stoneleigh Abbey (*above*), set in the midst of a well-wooded, fertile park through which the Avon leisurely winds its course, has behind it a history of over eight centuries. For it was in 1154 that land here was first granted to a small community of Cistercian monks, who established in the years that followed one of the most prosperous abbeys of medieval England. From the middle of the sixteenth century the property has belonged to the Leigh family.

Apart from certain remains incorporated in the later mansion, nothing survives of the original structure of the abbey except the Gatehouse (*right*) described by Dugdale as a 'fair and strong' building. It was built by Abbot Richard de Hockele in 1346, three years before the Black Death, and still serves its original purpose as a gatehouse, controlling access to the house beyond. The present classical mansion which incorporates an Elizabethan house erected by Sir Thomas Leigh on the site and ruins of the medieval abbey was designed by Francis Smith of Warwick about 1720.

COVENTRY

To countless thousands mention of the name of Coventry recalls that in 1940 the city underwent one of the most vicious air raids of the Second World War, during which St Michael's Cathedral was destroyed and the central area of the city devastated to such an extent as to make its almost complete rebuilding necessary. Up till that time Coventry's streets and buildings had retained much of their medieval character and appearance and visitors had been surprised to find so much of the old and picturesque in so famous a centre of industry. Only a few buildings such as Ford's Hospital (*below*), seriously damaged by enemy bombs but since restored, remain to serve as a reminder of the former charm and beauty of this ancient city of spires. This sixteenth-century timber-framed hospital was founded in 1529 by William Ford, merchant of Coventry, and William Pisford, and has served as an almshouse from the time of its building. Bond's Hospital, near to St Johns Church, is a similar foundation.

In contrast Coventry's new city centre, with its many public and commercial buildings, is strikingly modern in design and conception. A traffic-free precinct in the centre (*opposite lower right*) has created a haven for the pedestrian and forms the central shopping area. Perhaps one of the best known personalities from Coventry's past is Lady Godiva, whose statue stands in Broadgate (*top right*). She was the wife of Leofric, Earl of Mercia who founded the Benedictine monastery in Coventry in the year 1043, around which the city grew. Legend has it that she rode naked through the streets as a protest against the heavy local taxes imposed by her husband.

The city's most outstanding single building is its new cathedral, designed by Basil Spence in a bold modern style incorporating contemporary materials and embellishments which contrast strongly with the traditional pattern of ecclesiastical architecture. It possesses many striking features, not the least of which are the Epstein bronzes of St Michael and the Devil by the main entrance (*top right*). The interior gives an impression of light and space and on entry the eye is drawn to the superb tapestry of Christ designed by Graham Sutherland (*below right*). The new cathedral contains a wealth of artistic contributions by contemporary artists.

GODIVA

WHEN SHE RODE BACK CLOTHED ON WITH
CHASTITY SHE TOOK THE TAX AWAY AND
BUILT HERSELF AN EVERLASTING NAME

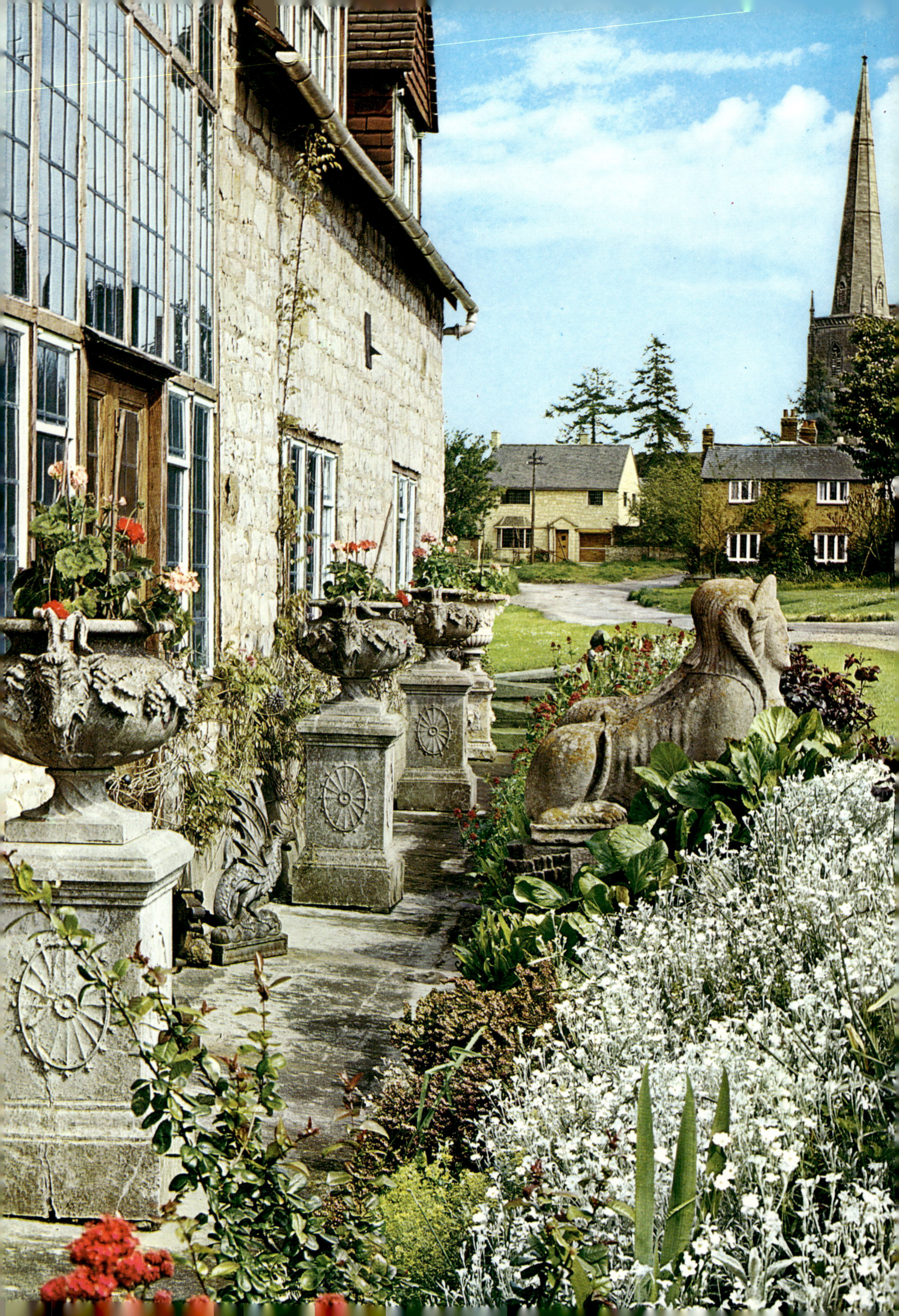

THE STOUR VILLAGES

Dotted along the valley of the River Stour upstream from its junction with the Avon, just south of Stratford, the villages of Clifford Chambers, Preston-on-Stour, Alderminster and Newbold-on-Stour, offer typical examples of beautiful churches, charming country cottages or impressive mansions characteristic of the Shakespeare country. Alscot Park, with its eighteenth-century mansion, is particularly attractive.

To the west on the Stour lies Tredington (*left*), a delightful grey stone village possessing an extremely interesting church with a very impressive steeple. Parts of the fabric date back to about the year AD 1000. The remains of two Anglo-Danish doorways which appear about thirteen feet above ground level, were originally approached by external wooden steps, leading to an internal gallery, which could be removed when required as a defence against marauding Danes. Galleries of this kind existed in pre-Conquest churches as, for example, at Jarrow in County Durham. This church was also involved in hostilities during the Civil War, and evidence of the impact of bullets in its 400-year-old wooden door may still be seen. The church has a splendid Jacobean pulpit and monuments of several periods.

A short distance to the south of Tredington lies the pretty village of Honington (*above*). Here the Stour is crossed by a five-arched bridge which has twenty-two stone balls lined up along the parapet. The village itself is delightfully set in parkland around a village green, with its main street unobtrusively hidden away. The village appears to have grown around Honington Hall, described by Nikolaus Pevsner as 'a gem of a late seventeenth-century house', built in 1682 by Sir Henry Parker, a wealthy London merchant. Very close to the Hall stands the Church of All Saints, mainly dating from the seventeenth century but with a thirteenth-century tower.

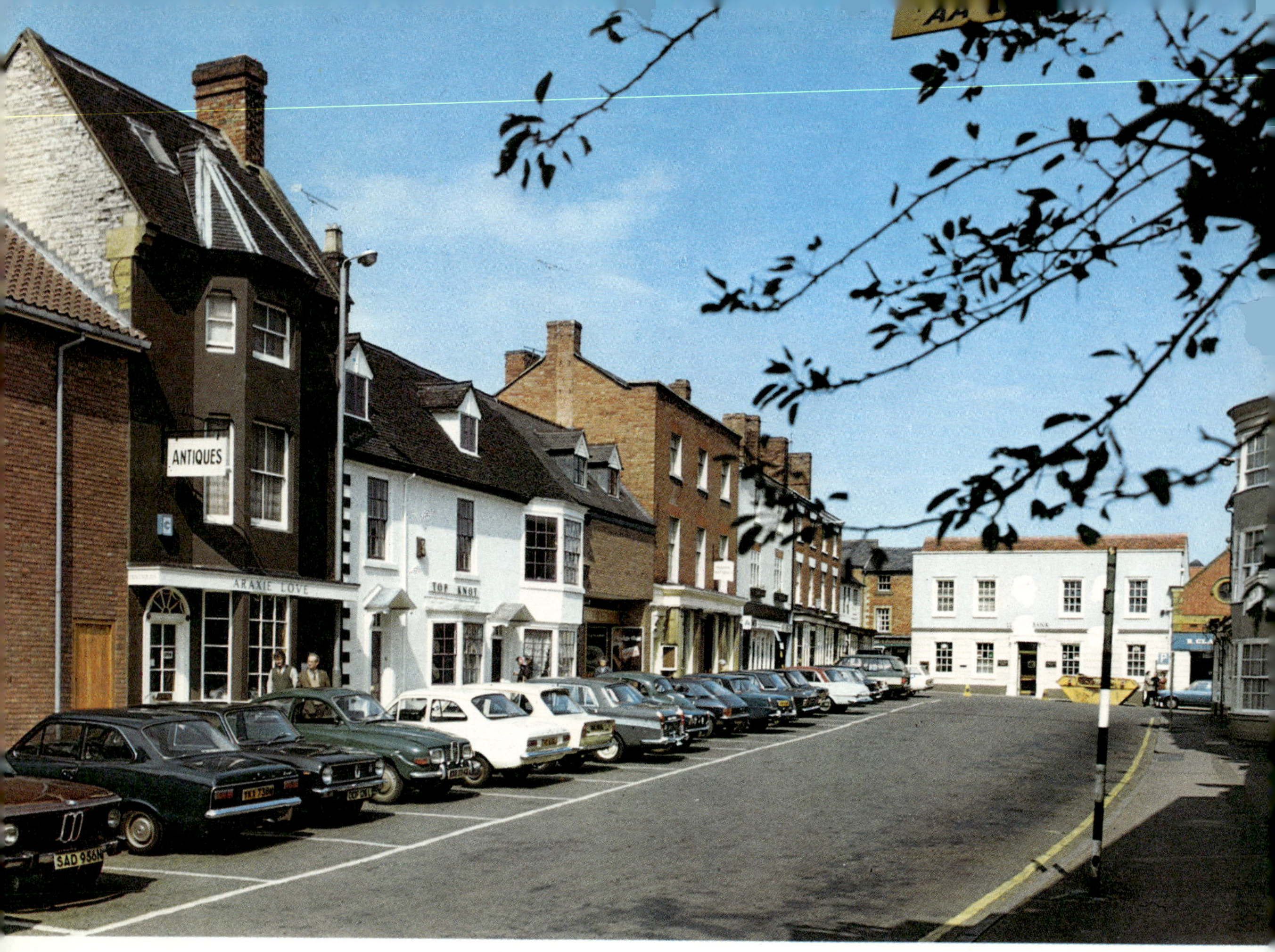
ANTIQUES
ARAXIE LOVE
TOP KNOT
SAD 956N

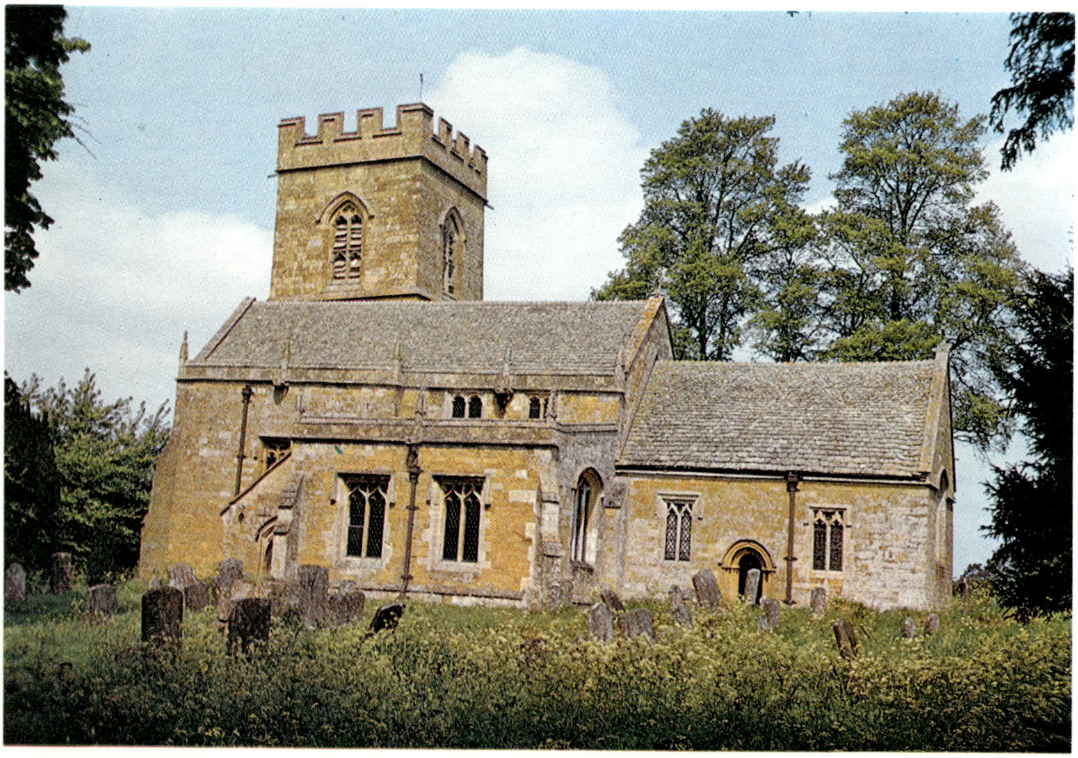

SHIPSTON-ON-STOUR

Typical of the small market towns which owed their original prosperity to sheep and the wool trade Shipston-on-Stour (*opposite top*) is situated on the main road from Stratford to Oxford on the borders of the Cotswold country. Its unpretentious buildings present a pleasing medley of architectural styles, with a few particularly fine Georgian houses and inns, reflecting the homely development of a small trading community over a period of centuries. Of special interest are the George Hotel of early Georgian date and the Horseshoes Inn with timber-framed upper floor. The nineteenth-century church with its fifteenth-century brown stone tower stands close by the side of Church Street which being a main road now carries heavy motor traffic. Parallel with this is High Street, a short wide street of considerable character closed at both ends. The Quaker meeting house in Church Street is one of the oldest in Warwickshire, about 1689.

WARWICKSHIRE CHURCHES

The Shakespeare country is liberally endowed with fine churches, with small villages often supporting quite substantially sized edifices. In the case of Barcheston (*opposite below*) just outside Shipston-on-Stour the small community which supported the church has all but disappeared except the Manor House. It was here that William Sheldon started his tapestry weaving in 1560.

Even more striking is the church of Wootton Wawen (*below*) situated on the main road to Birmingham between Stratford and Henley-in-Arden. It is said to be the oldest church in Warwickshire, with a Saxon foundation. The church is also notable for its contents, which include a beautiful fifteenth-century carved oak screen and pulpit, two old chests ornamented with wrought iron, a desk with ancient books chained to it, and several particularly fine brasses and monuments. The interior is a mixture of many different styles.

COMPTON WYNYATES

Compton Wynyates (*above*), probably England's most beautiful manor house, is situated in an unusually lovely setting in a dip of the wooded hills and is approached by narrow lanes. Built in the reign of Henry VIII, with later additions, the buildings are grouped round a quadrangle. Nowhere have bricks, timber and stone been fused into a more perfect architectural composition combining rare beauty of proportion and design with the natural advantages of such an exceptional site.

The mansion belongs to the Marquis of Northampton and was mainly built by his ancestor Sir William Compton in the early sixteenth century. Comptons had been lords of the manor here as far back as before the Magna Carta. The house is rich in historical associations. As a boy Sir William was page to the future Henry VIII, who visited the house several times in later years. The arms of Henry VIII and Katherine of Aragon are still over the porch. During the Civil War Compton Wynyates was occupied by Parliamentary troops, after strong resistance from the fiercely royalist Comptons. Despite the destruction of the nearby church and the filling in of the moat, the house itself was not damaged. More than a century later this beautiful mansion narrowly escaped demolition by the eighth Earl of Northampton, who acquired massive debts from an extravagant parliamentary election campaign. Fortunately his agent, John Berrill, merely bricked up the windows and the house was repaired and reoccupied nearly seventy years later by the second Marquis.

The inside of the house abounds in interesting architectural features and reminders of its fascinating past: the great hall with its original timbered roof and minstrel gallery; the chapel with its carved screen depicting the seven deadly sins; the priest's chamber; secret passages and hiding places; and the stately rooms with their fine panelling and plasterwork, all containing furniture and paintings of equal charm.

The garden is particularly noteworthy for its fantastically shaped yew trees and hedges.

BROUGHTON CASTLE

Broughton Castle (*below*), southwest of Banbury on the road to Shipston-on-Stour, is also rich in historical connections, spreading over six centuries. In 1306 a fortified stone manor house was erected by Sir John Broughton. At the death of the last of his heirs, the property was bought by William de Wykeham, founder of Winchester School and New College, Oxford. In 1405 Thomas Wykeham converted the building into a castle with battlements and a gatehouse. Through marriage the estate passed into the Fiennes family, by whom it is still owned and occupied. During the sixteenth century they carried out substantial additions and changes, by removing battlements, adding stories and huge mullioned windows, inserting a beautiful plaster ceiling in the Great Hall, and generally turning an uncomfortable medieval castle into the pleasant Tudor building that can be seen today.

Perhaps the best known member of the family was Sir William Fiennes, who gained a reputation for subtlety and shrewdness during the Civil War and was one of the few leading Parliamentarians to emerge unscathed from the years of political upheaval.

The castle was built on an artificial island, its moat created by a blocked-up stream and now covered by water lilies. This peaceful setting among woods and water must surely make it one of the most beautifully situated English castles.

EVESHAM

Evesham is a homely, busy market town, the centre of the Vale of Evesham vegetable and fruit growing industry. Apart from its calm stretch of river, the town presents a pleasing medley of architectural styles of all periods, including picturesque inns, some splendid Georgian houses, and half-timbered black-and-white buildings such as the Booth Hall (*below left*) in the Market Place. This building dates from the late fifteenth century. Once its lower floor was used as a covered market while town meetings took place upstairs but, by Tudor times, the town had expanded so much that the Booth Hall proved too small and the Guildhall was built in its stead.

The medieval Benedictine Abbey of Evesham was founded in 714 but all that survives is the Norman gateway of the churchyard and the fifteenth-century Bell Tower (*below and left*). The Bell Tower was built by Abbot Lichfield, the last of Evesham's abbots, just before the Dissolution. It is some 110 feet high and has exquisitely ornamented buttresses and pinnacles, and is one of the finest examples of late Perpendicular work in this country. At the Dissolution of 1539, the earlier abbey buildings were destroyed but the Bell Tower was fortunately left intact.

HIDCOTE MANOR GARDEN

Hidden away in the little hamlet of Hidcote Bartrim on the fringe of the Cotswolds, eleven miles to the southwest of Stratford-upon-Avon, is one of the most fascinating modern garden creations in England. Major Lawrence Johnston, who gave the property to the National Trust in 1948, fashioned here around a manor house grounds of considerable beauty (*above*). The house itself dates from the seventeenth and eighteenth centuries.

The garden at Hidcote, laid out during the early years of the present century, is a succession of surprises. Here, a peep through a doorway in a yew hedge reveals yet another garden enclosure; there, a turning one way or the other opens up a long vista of grass or trees. Winding paths lead suddenly to restful, shady bowers; secluded shelters and terraces discover themselves in unexpected places; everywhere trees, shrubs and flowers, sometimes planted in severe formality, and sometimes in delightful informality, combine to produce an atmosphere of utter peace.

Not only are the extensive grounds of Hidcote Manor a constant source of pleasure to all avid gardeners and lovers of nature, but they are also greatly appreciated by botanists. Here, rare plants can grow in abundance since they are sheltered from excessive rain and wind by the many trees and steep banks. Indeed, so much botanical work has been carried out here that several plants now incorporate 'Hidcote' in their names.

THE SHAKESPEARE VILLAGES

Within easy reach of Stratford on the west lies a group of pretty villages and hamlets with traditional claims to Shakespearian associations, linked together in the well-known doggerel verse:

*Piping Pebworth, dancing Marston,
Haunted Hillborough, hungry Grafton,
Dodging Exhall, Papist Wixford,
Beggarly Broom and drunken Bidford.*

These villages are Pebworth, Long Marston, Hillborough, Temple Grafton, Exhall, Wixford, Broom and Bidford-on-Avon. Other villages of similar character merge the Shakespeare country into the Cotswold area.

According to a rather dubious legend, the men of the village of Bidford-on-Avon prided themselves on their drinking ability and issued challenges to all-comers to join them at the Falcon Inn. A contingent from Stratford, including the redoubtable Mr Shakespeare, took up the challenge, only to be thwarted by the local champions. The gallant losers apparently only managed half a mile of the return journey before collapsing under a crab-apple tree. Shakespeare is reputed to have composed the above ditty upon being aroused from his somewhat deep slumber.

Many of these villages are still approached through country lanes and although they are no longer isolated as in earlier times, they still retain all the essential characteristics of rural life. Old-world stone and thatched cottages in delightful gardens, such as the one at Hidcote Bartrim (*above*), still add atmosphere and charm to the scene.

Apart from the fame of its Falcon Inn

Bidford-on-Avon (*below*) is notable for its narrow medieval bridge with eight irregular arches and for its church occupying a commanding position alongside the river. The village originated as a river-crossing settlement: Icknield Way ran through here in Roman times and later the Anglo-Saxon invaders settled here. Some years ago over 200 burials were excavated; the weapons, ornaments and household objects excavated provided important archaeological evidence concerning the customs of these early settlers.

Weston-on-Avon is yet another pretty village lying on the banks of this beautiful river. Many of the houses and cottages here are thatched, including Weston Court (*above*). Behind can be seen All Saints Church, remarkable for its array of closely built north windows, dating from the fifteenth century. It also contains excellent brasses, particularly of Sir John Grevill (1547), in armour, bearded and wearing broad shoes.

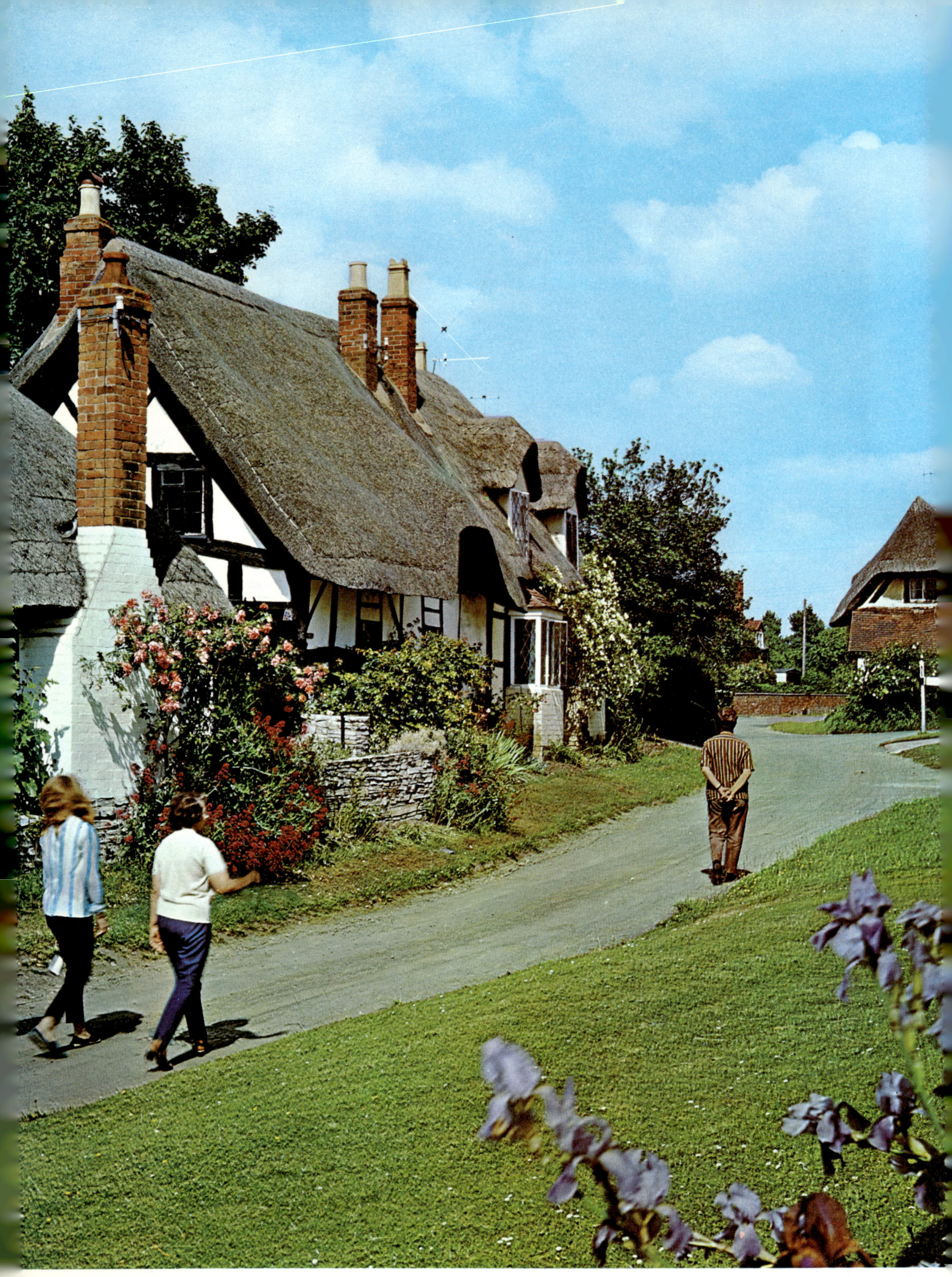

WELFORD-ON-AVON

Lying between Stratford and Bidford-on-Avon, the riverside village of Welford is one of the prettiest places in the Shakespeare country. The Avon, spanned by a grand old bridge, is particularly lovely here and the scattered village streets are lined with well-kept cottages surrounded by gardens, fruit orchards and market-garden plots. In blossom and fruit time Welford is especially attractive.

Boat Lane (*left*), with its timber and white-washed, thatched cottages, its trim grass verges and colourful flowers, excels in picturesque effect. It leads down to the river and its name is reminiscent of the days when boats were drawn up here on the bank. From the lane an oak lych-gate shows the way to a particularly beautiful church, containing many Norman features. The stonework of the tower and nave, formerly covered with rendering, has now been restored to its original appearance, while gravestones in the churchyard provide evidence of the age of the church. Until recently Welford still had a mill just as it did in Shakespeare's day, and it is one of the few villages left which preserves its maypole, painted in traditional colours, on its village green.

THE COTSWOLDS: BOURTON-ON-THE-WATER

Within easy reach of Stratford-upon-Avon are the beautiful old-world towns and villages built of mellowed yellow stone that harmonise with the peculiarly unspoilt English countryside of the Cotswold Hills. Indeed, Shakespeare's country merges imperceptibly into the undulating Cotswold country.

This area is well watered with springs, brooks, and small rivers which glide through villages and hamlets, past cottage, farm and church. The River Windrush flows with its clear shallow water, spanned by graceful bridges, through the very centre of Bourton-on-the-Water (*above*), which has now become the Cotswolds' most spectacular beauty spot. Indeed, at certain times its beauty is now threatened by over-popularity. The village draws very many visitors in summer who find much of interest here, especially the model village at the rear of the New Inn. This is a remarkable model of Bourton itself, with each house faithfully represented to a scale of one-tenth, and it took six men four years to construct. Another attraction is 'Birdland', a fine ornithological collection of rare species.

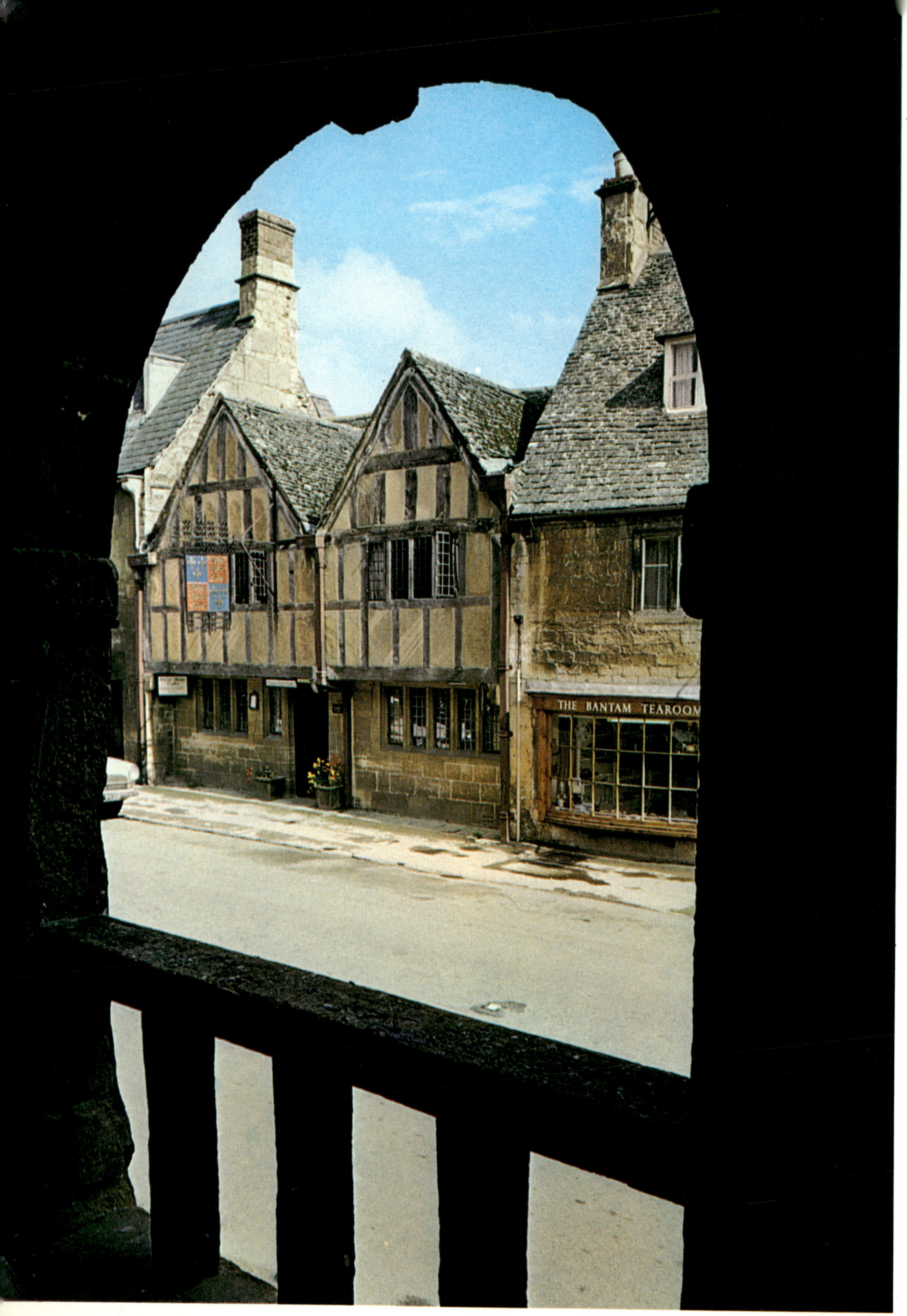
THE BANTAM TEAROOM

CHIPPING CAMPDEN

During the Middle Ages the rearing of sheep, with the resultant production of wool, brought great prosperity to the Cotswold region. The wool trade reached its zenith in the fifteenth century, when Chipping Campden (*left*) became one of the leading centres of the industry, and the town still reflects the affluence of that period.

Rich merchants built comfortable houses of the friendly local stone with such taste and good craftsmanship that many remain today to enhance the attractiveness of this town, and they still retain much of the leisured dignity of bygone ages. The buildings of Chipping Campden date from every century since the fourteenth, yet here the many varied styles do not appear to clash. They are practically all built of the same material – Cotswold stone, with its mellowed golden tints.

The long and curving High Street has been aptly described as the most beautiful street in Britain. Here stands Grevel's House, with its unusual two-storeyed bay window. The house, which was built about 1380 and is one of the oldest buildings in the town, once belonged to William Grevel, a prosperous wool merchant. Among the many other splendid structures here is the Wool Market Hall – the town has always had an important market while the prefix of 'Chipping' is derived from the Old English word for 'market'. The Hall dates from the Jacobean period and was built by Sir Baptist Hicks, a great benefactor to the town, whose coat of arms it still bears. He also built a group of attractive almshouses, raised above street level, in 1624.

Chipping Campden is dominated by the magnificent medieval church of St James (*above*), a predominantly Perpendicular edifice which was founded in late Norman times. It has been extensively rebuilt although a few Norman traces can still be distinguished. The main feature of the church, its elegant pinnacled and well-proportioned tower, was erected in the fifteenth century. The church contains one of the finest collections of ancient ecclesiastical vestments in the country, while many excellent brasses can also be examined here. One in particular commemorates William Grevel and it describes him as 'The flower of wool merchants of all England'. The brasses are set into the chancel floor, before the altar. In one side chapel, known as the Noel Chapel, is an impressive monument to Sir Baptist Hicks and his wife.

THE COTSWOLD HERITAGE

The tranquil village of Upper Slaughter, as yet untouched by modern industrial development, is situated on a lush green hillside just above Lower Slaughter. The shallow Eye, a clear stream which finds its way into the River Windrush eventually, flows through both these delightful villages. It is crossed by several simple footbridges – this photograph (*below*) shows the bridge at Upper Slaughter.

Typical Cotswold stone cottages and farm buildings are grouped around the stream but the focal point of Upper Slaughter is its fine Norman church, rebuilt during the Middle Ages, unusual in that it has two fonts. One of these, dating from the fifteenth century, was discarded sometime in the last century and thrown into the churchyard. A copy was made for use in the church but, fortunately, the original font was eventually rescued and replaced in its rightful position.

Upper Slaughter Manor House, tucked away among the hills, is one of the most beautiful and important architectural treasures in the Cotswolds. Most of this twelve-gabled edifice dates from Elizabethan times and, even though the two-storeyed porch is Jacobean, it harmonises perfectly with the earlier building.

BROADWAY

The most visited of all the Cotswold towns, Broadway is deservedly famous, for in many respects it epitomises the appeal of the whole area. As its name suggests, it has a very broad main street, bordered with ample grass verges studded with trees, which gradually rises towards the hills.

Broadway's stone-built cottages and shops are all characteristic of the local style of building, many being of sixteenth- and seventeenth-century date (*bottom*). Probably the most impressive building is the Lygon Arms, (*below*) situated at the lower end of the mile-long street. This is a hostelry of distinction and charm, built at the end of the fifteenth century, when it was known as the White Hart. It is reputed that both Charles I and Cromwell stayed here. The hotel today is graced with a lovely garden, while its courtyard is large enough to allow the local Meet to gather here before setting out on the hunt. Other houses of note include Court Farm, once the home of the famous Shakespearian actress Mary Anderson; Tudor House, Picton House, and the fourteenth-century Abbot's Grange, which once belonged to the Abbots of Evesham.

STANTON IN THE COTSWOLDS

Stanton, lying to the southwest of Broadway, is what might well be described as a classic Cotswold village situated in typical Cotswold countryside. It was mainly built in the early seventeenth century when the prosperity of the local yeoman farmers was at its height. The local masons seem to have used all their ingenuity with the warm Cotswold stone to create a variety of styles that still remain typical of the area. The village was fortunate not to fall prey to haphazard twentieth-century modernisation or demolition, for careful restoration was carried out early this century by Sir Philip Stott, an architect, who bought the estate containing most of the village in 1906.

Stanton church is Perpendicular in style with a tall, elegant spire, but the original church was Norman and a few remaining traces from this period are still visible.

The publishers acknowledge the Shakespeare Birthplace Trust and others for permitting the reproduction of the illustrations in this publication.

85306 634 5

© 1980 Jarrold Colour Publications, Norwich
Printed and bound in Great Britain
by Jarrold and Sons Ltd, Norwich 480

Front cover: Swans on the Avon.
Back cover: Chipping Campden, one of the many merchants' homes.
Inside covers: Shakespeare's Warwickshire.
John Speed's map of about 1610.